The
Conscious
Divorce

The Conscious Divorce

30 PRINCIPLES TO HELP YOU CHOOSE YOURSELF

Kristina Jay

O'LEARY
PUBLISHING
The Influencer's Press

NAPLES, FL

Published in the United States by
O'Leary Publishing
www.olearypublishing.com

The views, information, or opinions expressed in this book are solely those of the authors involved and do not necessarily represent those of O'Leary Publishing, LLC.

The author has made every effort possible to ensure the accuracy of the information presented in this book. However, the information herein is sold without warranty, either expressed or implied. Neither the author, publisher, nor any dealer or distributor of this book will be held liable for any damages caused either directly or indirectly by the instructions or information contained in this book. You are encouraged to seek professional advice before taking any action mentioned herein.

ISBN (print): 978-1-952491-29-0
ISBN (ebook): 978-1-952491-60-3
Library of Congress Control Number: 2021915014

Editing by Heather Davis Desrocher
Proofreading Kat Langenheim
Cover and interior design by Jessica Angerstein

Printed in the United States of America

To my daughter, my heart,
may you consciously choose a life of authenticity,
empowerment and unconditional love.

Contents

PHASE 3 The Process

PHASE 4 A New Beginning

Preface

Since my divorce in December of 2017, I have evolved so much as a woman and as a human being. However, I remember the pain, despair and heartbreak I felt during that time in my life when I was contemplating divorce; so it is with deep compassion and love for you that I am writing this book. I realize now that the best choice I could have made was when *I Chose Myself* and my well-being. This led to my decision to divorce, which was one of the most difficult decisions I have ever made. Overcoming my fear, guilt and shame was extremely challenging and felt almost impossible. However, with tremendous faith and courage, I moved forward and completed a successful divorce. I know that you can too, if that is what you choose.

The definition of a successful divorce is personal. To me it meant ending a marriage that no longer served my soul and doing it in a way that was full of grace, tact and compassion for myself, my former husband, and my daughter. To accomplish success, I used certain guiding *Principles* throughout the divorce process. These allowed me to complete a *Conscious Divorce,* with dignity, and with the least amount of pain and suffering for all involved. As my daughter would say, this helped me *turn lemons into lemonade!*

I have learned so much about myself and life through the experience of divorce. The woman who wrote this book is not the same woman who chose divorce four years ago. Divorce led me on a journey of empowerment as I searched for my spiritual Truth. Now, with continued spiritual growth, I wonder if the woman I am today could have prevented her divorce back then (although I was only half of the equation). I will never know, and I do firmly believe that we are exactly in the place we are meant to be. I also believe that we are all doing the best we can in each moment. So, it is my heartfelt hope that all I have learned, and now share with you in the pages of this book, will either help you execute a divorce with courage, faith, mindfulness and compassion, or support you in continuing your marriage journey in a new way. In either case, taking responsibility for yourself and the rest of your journey is what matters the most.

I used to believe that life was about finding yourself, but that was a journey that kept me looking outside of myself. Now I understand that life is about knowing your Truth and creating your experience, which comes from taking responsibility for yourself and your life – all of you and all of it. With responsibility you step into your power, directing your journey and creating it with intention and purpose – because above all, life is about consciously creating and evolving into a state of unconditional love for all.

I am still learning how to be a dynamic and responsible co-creator of my journey. It is with humility, vulnerability and reverence that I embrace life and it's lessons. It is with intention and faith that I consciously create a life I love. It is with acceptance and compassion that I will continue to love and care for myself, and most importantly, to *Choose Me!*

And so, I offer you this book with the hope that you too will *Choose Yourself.*

Introduction

This book is a book of *solutions.* After my journey through a successful divorce, I felt that I could best serve others and pay it forward by sharing these practical solutions, or *Principles*, that supported me throughout the process of divorce. These *Principles* allowed me to execute divorce in a mindful and conscious way. I have created this book to support you in doing the same.

My contemplation of divorce started with one *Principle*: *Choose Yourself!* With this *Principle*, I realized that my life was not in alignment with my soul's desires. This awareness, and many others, led me to take responsibility for my journey, to choose myself, and to make the decision to divorce.

There is an abundance of information available to anyone who is considering a divorce. That information may provide you with the appropriate steps for executing a divorce. However, I will provide you with what's missing – with what is not easily available. I will share with you the knowledge that only comes from personal experience – the pearls of wisdom and solutions that can only be shared by someone who has been there and executed a *Conscious Divorce* with dignity and grace.

Choosing to divorce is a life changing event for not just you, but for all family members involved. When I made a decision to divorce, I wanted to *Choose Me*, but I also wanted to *Choose Them*, my family. Because of this, I executed my divorce in the most mindful and conscious way possible. And you can too.

This book is divided into four phases of divorce: *The Decision, The Preparations, The Process,* and *A New Beginning*. There are a total of 30 *Principles* in this book spread over the four phases. These are the *Principles* that served me in consciously executing a successful divorce. By using these practical *Principles* to guide your divorce, you too will be able to have a successful outcome – one that includes dignity, self-respect and compassion for all involved.

You may become aware of the correlation between the four phases of divorce and life processes. Just as in divorce, in your life *decisions* you *prepare*, *process* and eventually come to a *new beginning*. In addition, after utilizing these 30 *Principles*, you may realize their universal nature and apply them to other life decisions and challenges. I continuously find power in applying these *Principles* to many areas of my life as I consciously *Choose Me*. Continuously choosing yourself becomes a daily journey – an evolution of self-love.

In the end, *The Conscious Divorce* is about taking responsibility for your life and choosing empowerment, self-love and freedom. I hope this book empowers you with more awareness of the Truth, power and freedom that lies within you. It's only a choice away. Have courage and faith because there is a light at the end of the tunnel – and that light is *you!*

30 Principles to

Help You
Choose
Yourself

The Serenity Prayer

*God grant me the **Serenity***

to accept the people I cannot change,

*The **Courage** to change*

the one I can, and

*The **Wisdom** to know it's me.*

The Decision

*You're always one decision away from
a totally different life.*

—Mark Batterson

The decision to divorce is not anything to take lightly. This first section contains a large number of the *Principles* because of the mindfulness that is required to make the most conscious decision for your marital circumstances. The decision to divorce requires awareness, contemplation and truth.

As you read through the *Principles* for *The Decision* to divorce phase, you will realize how they can assist you in finding clarity about your marriage and the courage to make a decision for change. The only thing that could be scarier than making a decision for change is the realization that nothing will change at all.

PRINCIPLE 1

Choose Yourself

Have the courage to take responsibility for
your own life journey.

The courage to choose yourself is the courage to choose responsibility for your life journey. One of the most challenging things about the decision to divorce is believing that you *do* have the right to end your marriage. The unknown can be intimidating and frightening. Fear can literally paralyze you from moving forward. When I came to the realization that only I could change my circumstances, I was terrified of this responsibility. But I was empowered at the same time. Was I going to remain in this "victim" state, blaming my circumstances on something outside of my control, or was I going to take responsibility for my life? I summoned the courage to take control of what was within my power – me! *I Chose Me*! I realized that no one was going to save me from my circumstances. Only I had the ability to do that – to make a decision and a change. So, with courage, I took action and moved forward with the decision to divorce.

Having the courage to choose myself and take responsibility for my journey revealed to me that we all have that right to choose ourselves, and therefore, *the responsibility* for our own journey. What freedom! It was even more liberating when I accepted that both my former husband's and my daughter's journeys were their own as well.

Choosing yourself and taking responsibility for your life is a gift of *empowerment and freedom* – for you as well as for those you love. You become empowered by allowing yourself the sole responsibility for your own journey, which in the end is freedom. In addition, you free others from this responsibility and allow them to remain empowered over their own journey.

So, take responsibility for your thoughts, beliefs and actions. You are powerful! Your choices matter and are yours to make and no one else's. Imagine a world where we are all empowered to live our best life because we allow each other to be responsible for our own journeys. That's freedom!

> *One of the most courageous decisions you'll ever make is to finally let go of what is hurting your heart and soul.*
>
> **—Brigette Nicole**

PRINCIPLE 2

Contrast Helps Clarity

Experiencing what you do not want brings more clarity about what you do want.

When we experience events or moments in life that we do not desire – *contrast* – it only provides us with more information about what we do desire. It reveals what is important to us. So, although "undesirables," or contrast, can be challenging and sometimes devastating, it does serve us. As Abraham Hicks explains in *Infinite Intelligence*, the more quickly we recognize and learn from contrast, the more quickly we can change direction, pivot towards what we *do* desire, and suffer less from the experience.

Before I made a decision to divorce, I experienced many emotional lows. I stayed in a marriage that was clearly not serving my soul for quite some time. I lived many moments that I knew were not how I wanted to live; and I was becoming a woman who I did not want to be. Therefore, I asked myself some difficult questions to clarify what needed to change. The dysfunction and heartache in the last few years of my marriage showed me what I did not desire; and it eventually led me towards the clarity of what I did desire: peace, joy, self-love and self-respect. I then made deliberate choices to move in the direction of what I desired.

Experiencing painful contrast is extremely effective in showing us what we *do not* want in life, and therefore revealing what we *do* want. It is a part of life that we cannot avoid. The key is to allow the contrast to help us understand and tune into our desires, instead of remaining focused on the contrast that we do not desire. With greater awareness in our lives, we can respond more consciously to contrast, instead of waiting for instability to demand our attention and force us into change. The perceived "problem" of contrast can reveal the answers you seek. Allow contrast to reveal what needs to change in your life. Allow it to give you the gift of clarity about what truly matters and what you desire. Then you will make choices that *align* with your desires.

Clarity is a consequence of holding your confusion consciously.

—Sadhguru

PRINCIPLE 3

What You Resist Persists

When you resist the reality of something in your life, you only strengthen it.

I was in an unhappy marriage for many years, but the last thing I wanted to do was to admit to myself that I was miserable. So, I enjoyed many distractions and denied the truth of my situation for as long as possible – parties, drinking, shopping, socializing, traveling, various committees, exercise, movies, etc. Whatever I could do in excess to distract me from my undesired reality, I did it! It wasn't until my soul was literally aching inside from resisting the truth of my reality that I gave awareness to it. We live in a society designed for denial and distraction. However, I know that when our soul wants our attention on something, that nagging feeling will not go away. The pull towards what we refuse to look at will only grow in intensity until we cave from the suffering of resisting it.

I finally stopped fighting the awareness of what was going on in my life and allowed myself to face it. Ultimately, I had suffered enough and had to address not only my marriage, but also, all behaviors, habits and situations that were not serving me. Only then, by letting go of the resistance to what my soul knew I needed, did my suffering begin to diminish.

There are so many times in life when we think it may be easier to ignore the reality of our lives and resist taking responsibility. However, the awareness of the undesired reality will only increase, as will our internal suffering. Only when we find the courage to face and accept what we have been ignoring will we have the power to address and change it. Then we can focus our thoughts and energy on the changes we want to make. Our soul knows what serves us best.

So, if it calls us towards something, we should trust its calling.

> *Whatever you fight you strengthen,*
> *and what you resist, persists.*
>
> **—Eckhart Tolle**

PRINCIPLE 4

Acceptance Is the Gateway to True Change

*Acceptance of your reality empowers you
to transform it.*

When I began having difficulties in my marriage, I remained in a state of denial for quite some time, not wanting to accept that my marriage was in trouble. However, when I accepted my circumstances, I found the power to change them. Once I took responsibility for my marital situation,

I realized that true transformation could only come from controlling what I could control – me! I understood that continuing or ending my marriage was my choice, and I would be the one living with the results of my choice. In all honesty, this motivated and empowered me, but also scared me.

When we don't accept or take ownership of our "stuff," our stuff owns us! We all have situations or circumstances in our lives that need to change, yet many of us find ourselves dodging this responsibility because we do not want to accept reality. We may believe that undesired circumstances will magically disappear when we ignore them, but that is rarely the case. There are usually two outcomes. One, you accept that there is a situation that needs addressing, take responsibility for it, accept power over it, and change it. Or two, you do not accept that there is a situation that needs addressing, do not take responsibility for it, gain no power over it, and nothing changes (at least not for the better). Either way, *you* will live with the results of *your* choice.

Acceptance of everything that transpires during and after a divorce comes in stages. I still find myself going through moments of transformation as I accept that I am actually divorced and adjust to the changes that have taken place in my life. Each time I accept one of these changes, I feel myself evolving.

Acceptance is a continuous and empowering choice in our lives. We give ourselves power over that which we accept. When we do not accept a situation, it becomes worse and we give it power over us. So, choose acceptance and take ownership of your life. Only then do you become empowered to make positive changes and transform your experience.

> *Accept then act. Whatever the present moment contains, accept it as if you had chosen it. Always work with it, not against it. This will miraculously transform your whole life.*
>
> **—Ekhart Tolle**

PRINCIPLE 5

Blaming Disempowers You

---

*When you blame someone else
you give them your power.*

Blaming is one of the easiest things to do – it comes so naturally to us. It was something I did in my marriage; yet it was also one of the most disempowering actions for me.

After many years of an unhappy marriage, I started blaming my former husband for my unhappiness. However, when I blamed him, I also gave him power over my happiness. I was assigning him responsibility for my happiness.

Blame is a way of trying to shift responsibility to someone else for our feelings and experiences. When we blame another person, we essentially give them all of the power and therefore believe that we have no power over our own situation. We disempower ourselves.

We take control of our lives when we stop blaming others for our feelings and problems. We empower ourselves as the one accountable for our own experiences and solutions. The amount of power we have is directly proportional to the amount of responsibility we take. And, the amount of resentment we feel for an individual is directly proportional to the amount of blame we place on him or her. By taking responsibility for our lives, we are claiming power over our lives.

I came to understand that I had to stop blaming my former husband and start taking responsibility for my happiness. I couldn't change him – and even my efforts to change myself *for him* were futile. I now understood that I could only control myself. So, when I stopped blaming him for my undesired circumstances, it empowered me to look within for answers – instead of excuses. It empowered me to make a change – *for myself* – instead of remaining a powerless victim. I accepted that I was the one responsible for, and in control of, my circumstances.

So, what would make me happy? What would make things better? Only I could know and only I could change what I was doing. I could only control myself. So I did. No more blaming. No more victimhood. *Happiness truly is an inside job!*

You may succeed in making another feel guilty about something by blaming him; but you won't succeed in changing whatever it is about you that is making you unhappy.

—Wayne Dyer

PRINCIPLE 6

Live Authentically

_____

Authenticity is being the person that your soul
desires, and living the life you want to live.

There is nothing worse than living an inauthentic life. Most of the time we are not even aware that we are doing it – until we have suffered enough to pay attention.

When my marriage became a relationship that I could not accept, and one where I no longer felt empowered, I became a self-destructive, miserable person. I lost my way; and didn't know how I had become the person I was. I was not living a life of integrity or authenticity. It became a charade – a self betrayal. I no longer had self-respect. I was no longer choosing myself. This just added to the compounding pain in my soul that was directing me to make a change in my life. I knew I had to be true to myself once more and so I made the decision to divorce.

Soon after the completion of my divorce I got a tattoo of birds in flight. Someone asked me if it symbolized freedom from marriage – it did not. The birds symbolized my freedom from inauthenticity. I was no longer going to be anyone other than the woman I wanted to be – a woman of integrity, authenticity and wholeness. I chose acceptance and self-love. *I Chose Me!*

So often in life we can veer off track from who we want to be in this world. When we engage in behavior or make choices that pull us further from ourselves and our integrity, we are abandoning our authentic selves. If we are wise enough to listen to our soul's calling – our intuition or our self correcting GPS system – we can live authentically and remain on the path that is meant for us. The more we love and respect ourselves and hold ourselves accountable for our experience, the more power, joy, freedom and purpose we will experience on our life journey.

Loving someone else should never require abandoning ourselves in the process. Love is where we go to become more of who we are, not less.

—Mark Groves

Life Is Happening in the Present Moment

The only moment that truly exists
is the present moment.

For many years I did not live in the present moment. Maybe this was because reality was too painful and I preferred not to see it. Instead, I spent a lot of time reliving and correcting the past. I was full of judgement, blame and frustration. Alternatively, I would focus on the stress and anxiety of the future. I was full of "if onlys," "should haves" and "what ifs." I was full of fear and little joy. Who can feel vitality when they are not really living? Who can change their reality when they have not faced it?

This type of existence was exhausting, depressing and futile. Being focused on the past or anxious about the future became so stressful that I had to change. I finally freed myself from this pattern of thinking when I came across *Eckhart Tolle's* insights about the present moment. I realized the following:

The past was gone. It only existed in my mind and was kept alive by my thoughts and perceptions of it. I realized that the same was true about the future. The future is always coming and never really arrives because by the time I experience it, it is now the present. So, the additional stress and anxiety caused by focusing on the past or the future was misplaced energy. The past and the future were out of my immediate control. The only control I really had was in the *present moment*. The moment that I was currently living was all that truly existed. I understood that I needed to remain present in order to change the reality that I no longer wanted.

When I allowed myself to remain in the present moment and feel what it had to offer, I was at peace! Clarity, freedom, happiness and power all lie within the present moment and arrive when we remove the distractions – the burdens of our past and the worry about our future. It's in the present moment that we perceive reality with a new clarity and see its possibilities to become anything we want it to be. It's the key to being a co-creator of your reality and it allows you to *enjoy the journey*, which is the continuous present moment.

When I finally became present, I knew that I needed to choose divorce. For so long I ran from the present moment because I did not want to feel the truth of my marriage. However, when I finally allowed myself to live in the present moment, I found clarity and became empowered to change my life. Living in the present provided me with power, choice and the freedom to go forward and live a life that I love. Living in the present moment can allow you to do the same.

The point of power is always in the present moment.

—Louise Hay

PRINCIPLE 8

You Can't Lose What Truly Matters

You will always have everything that you
will ever need inside of you.

One of the scariest things about divorce is the unknown! While contemplating the decision to divorce, I remember the long list of fears that ran through my mind over and over again – from financial instability and a lifestyle change to family obligations – from the loss of friends to the judgement of others. Who was I going to be after divorce changed my reality? What would my new life look like after a life I had co-created for over 20 years with the same man no longer existed? There were so many unknown factors; and as each moment took me closer to the decision to divorce, I became more petrified.

My moment of clarity and courage came when I realized that I had already experienced many changes in my life and so much growth. I was not going to lose those experiences or that growth. I was not going to lose the people who truly loved me and whom I loved. I was not going to lose all of my wonderful memories. I was not going to lose my ability to love. I was not going to lose my intelligence or my ability to live in integrity and authenticity. I might even gain more of this. I was not going to lose my potential and ability to create a life that I love. *I was not my circumstances! I was not my "stuff" or the roles I played! I was not what I had identified with! I was so much more! I was not going to lose my true-self!* It was a brief, yet powerful, moment of clarity. It was a moment of seeing my true-self and unconditional self-love.

Sometimes in life, it takes hitting rock bottom to realize the Truth of who we really are, what really matters, and what we are capable of accomplishing. These moments of vulnerability can reveal to us that *we are enough* just as we are. Nothing outside of ourselves shows us who we are; it's realized only from within. This was the gift of a seemingly tragic event. Your experience may reveal this gift to you as well, and many more, if you allow it.

> *You already have everything you need to be content. Your real work is to do whatever it takes to realize that.*
>
> **—Geneen Roth**

PRINCIPLE 9

Be the Example

We teach others who we are with our actions.

Actions speak louder than words. Our actions really do show others who we are; they define our character. I have always known this; but it wasn't until my divorce that this actually came to have a deeper meaning for me.

One of the most complicated parts about the decision to divorce is the well-being of our children. I read many articles comparing the adverse effects on children of dysfunctional homes versus the effects of having co-parenting, divorced parents. I researched the short versus long-term effects of both situations, as well as data on how divorce can affect children differently depending upon their age. It is a complicated part of the decision process. At least for me it was! The guilt and loving obligation to my daughter was overwhelming. This one aspect alone contributed to my delaying the decision to divorce.

However, at one point I had an epiphany in the form of a question. "What would I tell my daughter to do if she was in this exact situation?" The answer suddenly seemed so clear. I would tell her that her happiness and well-being was what mattered and that she should do what was best for her! She should take responsibility for her well-being and create the life she desires.

Aha! Why was it okay in this hypothetical scenario for me to grant my daughter support and encouragement to *choose herself* – yet I was not able to give myself permission to do the same? As parents, particularly mothers, we so often do not give our own journey the same value as that of our children's. I concluded that this was *my* journey; therefore, I needed to make choices for myself and what my soul needed. My daughter would have her own journey and her own choices to make. In addition, at that time, I could not be the mother that my daughter deserved. I needed to take care of my well-being. In other words, I needed to, "put my oxygen mask on first before I could help her." This is the difference between self-love and selfishness. Self-love empowers all. Selfishness only empowers the ego. I needed to give myself permission to choose self-love, to *Choose Me* – and I did! With this decision, I was also *Choosing Her!*

I hoped that one day my daughter would respect me for being true to myself and for taking responsibility for my own happiness and my own journey. I was showing her how to respect and love herself. I came to the conclusion that my job as a mother was to invite my daughter to be part of my journey, and to be the example of a woman she could be proud of and respect. I had to assume responsibility for my *highest* responsibility – myself.

In the end, I made decisions that empowered and honored me, and that, by example, would give my daughter permission to do the same in her own life. I hope my daughter will always have the courage to *Choose Herself.*

When it comes to anyone in life – not just our children – we are continuously showing people who we are through our actions more than anything else.

Our actions are also an example to others of what is possible. The example of our journey provides others with a blueprint of lessons, and the permission to choose themselves in new ways. Choosing a life of courage and integrity is something in which we can take pride. May you have courage and also *Be the Example* in your life!

> *The world is changed by your example,*
> *not by your opinion.*
>
> **—Paulo Coelho**

Use the ABCs of Decision Making

Awareness, Beliefs and Choices support Decisions.

As with all decisions in your life, the decision to divorce must be made in the most mindful, conscious and aware state possible. The *ABCs of Decision Making* is a process that assists you in making conscious decisions.

Awareness

The *ABCs* start with *Awareness* – you can't change that of which you are not aware. Awareness is seeing all aspects of your situation for what they really are, without your stories or embellishments. In awareness, allow yourself to witness the truth of your situation. Contemplate these questions – write them down – and allow yourself time to know your truth:

What do I see taking place in my marriage?

How do I treat my spouse?

How am I treated by my spouse?

How does my marriage feel to me? - What feels wrong? - What feels right?

Does my spouse know how I feel?

Do I know how my spouse feels?

Are there outside influences affecting our marriage?

Am I happy in my marriage?

Am I still in love with my partner?

Beliefs

Once you have gained more awareness of the truth of your marriage, then it is time to look at your *Beliefs*. Awareness is about your observation, senses and feelings. Beliefs are the repetitive thoughts you have about your situation. Beliefs are powerful.

They can empower you or they can limit you, as they are the impetus for your choices and actions. Therefore, question if your beliefs are true or if they are assumptions. Some of the questions to ask yourself are:

What do I believe about the state of my marriage?

Can my marriage be improved?

What is preventing my marriage from being successful?

Have I done all that I can to fix it?

What do I still love about my marriage? Anything? What is working?

Do we need counselling?

Am I seeing the truth of my relationship or telling myself stories?

Am I blaming others?

Am I taking responsibility for my faults?

Do I want to stay in my marriage?

Can I be happy in my marriage?

Is my soul able to grow and be at peace in my marriage?

Am I still in love?

Is there anything more that I need to know about my present circumstances in order to make a decision about divorce?

These are questions to help you determine what you believe about your marriage and its current state.

Choices

Choices is the next phase in the *ABCs of Decision Making.* Once you have sifted through and examined your beliefs about the state of your marriage, you may now have a better ability to address the choices you make next.

Will I stay? Will I divorce?

Do I need more time to decide through contemplation or counselling?

Will I continue on in my marriage with a different approach?

Only you can make your choice and live the results of your choice. No one can do this for you.

When I chose to divorce it took me quite a while to find the courage to sit in *Awareness* of my situation, examine what I *Believed*, and make a *Choice* to divorce. It also involved counseling, contemplation and a lot of tears as I made my decision. I was emotionally confused because I still *believed* that I loved my husband, yet I didn't *feel* any love between us. This conflict told me that my relationship was no longer supporting my well-being. The *ABCs* helped me to move out of denial, confusion and fear, and along to a decision.

The ABCs of Decision Making is an effective *Principle* that supports you in making decisions. Freedom comes when you take responsibility for your life and make conscious choices. It comes when you say: *I Choose Me*!

> *May your choices reflect your hopes, not your fears.*
>
> **—Nelson Mandela**

The Preparations

The day a woman decides to divorce,
is not the day she leaves.

—Unknown

The Preparations phase of divorce is a logical and strategic process. Yet sometimes, when dealing with something as painful and emotional as divorce, we may overlook the value of strategic and preparatory actions.

Implementing these preparatory *Principles* will allow for a more mindful, strategic, and aligned divorce process. These *Principles* will support you for a more peaceful and successful outcome.

Let Your Faith Be Greater than Your Fear

Faith allows you to respond to life, fear does not.

Throughout my divorce I used this *Principle* multiple times a day. Faith gives you the courage to respond to and take care of everything that you need to in your life. It provides you with the confidence and awareness to do what it is that you need to do next – and even allows you to know when you need help in life. Faith allows you to be responsible for your journey – it is the belief in your spirit as a companion and guide. Faith is choosing the energy of love over fear. You activate faith by staying conscious and in the present moment. You activate faith by allowing yourself to be vulnerable.

This affirmation and belief, *Let your faith be greater than your fear,* provided me with courage while I was preparing for the divorce, as well as throughout the divorce process. There were many moments where fear could have stopped me from moving forward, giving up my intention to divorce. In a moment of fear, all efforts could have been easily abandoned. That is why this affirmation became so significant to me. It became my reminder to take deliberate actions and stay true to my intentions.

Fear hinders us in so many ways. It stops us from making intuitive, clear decisions and from taking action. Fear was the biggest challenge that I dealt with throughout the entire divorce process. I feared the unknown and what might be, or what may never be. Thankfully, with the continued support of this *Principle,* my level of faith and trust in myself has grown, along with my ability to consciously respond to my life, with deliberate action, rather than react to it.

As a friend once told me, "Life is constantly changing and you can't fear life!" So choose to continue evolving and become who you wish to be. Don't allow the fear of change and the unknown to stop you from creating what could be your best life ever. Have faith!

> *Faith is taking the first step even when you don't see the whole staircase.*
>
> **- Martin Luther King, Jr.**

Affirmations Allow Transformation

Affirmations allow us to become what we believe.

Preparing for a divorce can feel very lonely at times, with many opportunities to change our minds and run back to "the known" in fear of the "unknown." I found that reading certain daily affirmations renewed my courage and strengthened my spirit whenever I felt myself losing faith. Affirmations are especially helpful in a time when our privacy is crucial and we may feel a lack of outside support.

Affirmations are powerful because our thoughts are powerful. Our thoughts create our beliefs, feelings and behaviors. So, what better way to support positive beliefs, feelings and behaviors than with supportive and positive thoughts?

Affirmations such as the following supported me throughout my divorce, fostering faith in myself and my decisions:

Supportive Affirmations

Only you can change your life, no one can do it for you.

There is a difference between giving up, and knowing that you've had enough.

You are Braver than you believe, stronger than you seem, smarter than you think and loved more than you know.

Sometimes walking away has nothing to do with weakness and everything to do with strength.

You will find that you don't need to trust others as much as you need to trust yourself to make the right choices.

You're always one decision away from a totally different life.

Be not afraid, for I am with you.

Let your Faith be greater than your Fear.

Don't look back, you're not going that way.

It is what it is but it becomes what you make of it.

We cannot direct the wind, but we can direct our sails.

My peace is mine. I won't give anyone the power to take it away from me.

Have the courage to be kind.

There is always something to be thankful for.

Eventually all the pieces fall into place. Until then, laugh at the confusion, live for the moment and know that everything happens for a reason.

These, and other affirmations, greatly supported me in times of need. I encourage you to use these affirmations, as well as affirmations that speak to you, as a supportive tool throughout your divorce. Strategically place them so that they become a daily reminder of what you choose to believe. Keep choosing "glass-half-full" thoughts and keep your faith.

I have used positive affirmations in the most miraculous ways. I used the affirmations I needed most over and over until I was finally receptive to them and embraced their message. Then I would switch them out for new thoughts once I outgrew them.

The use and support of affirmations help shape our beliefs. They help us take responsibility for our attitude. We can use affirmations in a transformational way, helping us to evolve along our journeys. Are you *Allowing Affirmations to Transform* your beliefs? Ask yourself this often so you can choose positive and empowering thoughts!

> *It's the repetition of affirmations that leads to beliefs. And once that belief becomes a deep conviction, things begin to happen.*
>
> **- Mohammad Ali**

PRINCIPLE 13

Intentions Matter

Your intentions are your personal mission statement.

While preparing for my divorce, I found that I easily became overwhelmed and lost in thoughts of the unknown, which triggered my fear. I often sought relief by grounding myself, and mindfully focusing back on the present moment. My intentions were to be true to myself and my family. I realized that by organizing my thoughts and *writing* my intentions down, I was able to better ground and center myself throughout the divorce. What I wrote down became my guiding ideals, or my *Divorce Mission Statement,* and I referred to it regularly.

The *Divorce Mission Statement* is a roadmap of personal values for the divorce process. Your intentions will guide your actions and should be created in a conscious manner. I found that it is best to initiate actions in the divorce from these mindful intentions, unclouded by the inevitable emotions that show up throughout the process. My mission statement included the following:

Divorce Mission Statement

1. *I will seek the highest perspective in all circumstances.*
2. *I will conduct myself with dignity and grace.*
3. *I will determine what I can and cannot control and focus on what I can control.*
4. *I will protect and safeguard our daughter from the divorce and I will show her love and support throughout the entire process.*
5. *I will only seek enough financial support to start again and effectively take care of our daughter.*
6. *I will have love and compassion for myself during the divorce and listen to myself and my inner voice for the final decision on all matters.*

7. *I will use emotional intelligence to help maintain calmness, awareness, and the ability to effectively and successfully execute the divorce.*

8. *I will treat my spouse with compassion and consideration while maintaining discernment for my own well-being.*

Writing a *Divorce Mission Statement* is a great grounding tool for the process of divorce. It served me well during my emotional moments, as I mindfully re-grounded myself in my Truth.

Your *Divorce Mission Statement* will be relative to your personal intentions and needs.

Another benefit of referring to your *Divorce Mission Statement* is that it may help you prevent *self-sabotage*, which could hinder your efforts. Self-sabotage is simply the self-defeating and unconscious beliefs, actions and patterns in which we engage. Being mindful of your intentions will help to keep you more deliberate and conscious about your choices throughout your divorce.

Our intentions in life matter. They are the catalyst for our decisions and actions. Intentions reveal to us what our priorities are in life. Our intentions actually inform us about ourselves. When we are able to gain clarity about our intentions, we gain clarity about who we are. This gives us the opportunity to make more mindful, genuine and loving choices in life.

> *When our actions are based on good intentions, our soul has no regrets.*
>
> **- Anthony Douglas Wiliams**

PRINCIPLE 14

Seek a Higher
Perspective

———————

*When we see through the eyes of understanding,
our perspective is always changed.*

While I was preparing for my divorce there were so many moments when I became emotionally lost in the details of what had happened, leading up to my decision to divorce. I was focused on the minutia, the conversations, the interactions, the self-talk and the stories. This was all a distraction from what I was trying to accomplish. My overall goal was to leave a marriage that was no longer working, to gain my freedom. Remembering my goal helped me to view the entire process of divorce with new understanding and from a higher perspective. This higher perspective allowed me to remain focused on the bigger picture and not become derailed by my negative thoughts and emotions.

Seeking a higher perspective also supported me *during* my divorce, whenever I felt that I was being antagonized or manipulated. I would detach from the drama, and ask myself, *What truly matters in this scenario? What do I want to get out of this?* I would then pause and pull back from the situation, allowing myself to see it from a more objective perspective, with a new understanding. This increased my awareness and freed me from many unnecessary emotional tricks of the ego, both his and mine. Seeing from a higher perspective allowed my divorce to flow more smoothly and allowed me to remain faithful to my true intentions.

Seeking the highest perspective in all life scenarios is an effective way to gain clarity and preserve your energy. This supports you in creating an amazing life, instead of just reacting to it. When we react to people and situations in our lives, instead of responding consciously, we veer off course from what truly matters. Viewing situations from a broader and contextualized perspective allows us to see more of the truth of a situation. Then we are able to make decisions and respond to our lives from a place of more love and power.

> *If there is one life skill that everyone on the planet needs, it is the ability to think with critical objectivity.*
>
> **- Henry David Thoreau**

PRINCIPLE 15

Be Prepared

For all things in life, prepare yourself for success.

Be Prepared is such a basic *Principle* yet it is so important for success, not only in a divorce but also, for all ventures in life. Divorce requires preparation in order to execute it smoothly and successfully. You may not be able to prepare for the unknown, but there are basic preparations that can align you for greater success.

Through my divorce experience I found that I had to prepare for my security, as well as for what I was going to experience emotionally. The following areas of preparation are important for your security and peace of mind: *Financial Security, Physical Security, Health Plan, and Well-Being of the Children.* The other *Principles* in *The Preparations* phase help address the emotional aspects of divorce.

Financial Security

Making financial preparations for divorce is crucial. You will need to secure funds for the cost of the divorce itself (lawyer's retainer fee and total cost of the process), as well as for basic life expenditures.

In addition to financial preparations for the divorce, you may want to assess your current assets. Make copies of all financial documents and keep them for your records. You will need to prepare a Financial Affidavit that summarizes all income, expenses and assets.

I was fortunate enough to have an individual 401k (pre-marital asset) that I liquidated to help me afford my divorce. I also withdrew money from a joint account (which became inaccessible later in the divorce process) to ensure that I had financial stability throughout the year-long divorce process. In addition, I spent months securing copies of all records needed for the Financial Affidavit.

It is important to have a bank account and credit cards that are in your name only. In addition, you may want to research your individual credit "worthiness" for future financial purchases, and take any necessary steps to ensure your ability to be financially independent.

Lastly, you will need to decide, if you are not already working, if you will work after your divorce is complete. Even a low paying, part-time job can do wonders for your self-esteem and confidence, if you were financially dependent throughout your marriage, as I was. It's a good feeling to earn your own, independent money as you begin your new life.

Physical Security

Physical security relates to where you will be living during and after the divorce. During the divorce you want to make sure you feel safe and have a secure location to reside, whether it is your current home or a new location that feels more secure for you.

Both my former husband and I stayed in our marital residence with our daughter during our divorce. We gave each other space in order to function as peacefully as possible during the divorce process. Many times one of the spouses will be legally obligated to live elsewhere during this process. You may also want to start the process of researching where you will live after your divorce. It will be an easier transition for you if you have prepared ahead of time.

Health Plan

Make preparations for maintaining your health and that of your children before the divorce begins. The divorce process can be tedious and stressful, so complete all medical care, physical checkups, dental work, eye care, etc. ahead of time, for all of you.

Also allow yourself some pampering as part of your self-love and stress-reduction process for what is to come. Do this for yourself if possible. You need to be your own best friend during this process!

Lastly, research individual health coverage for after the divorce. You may or may not need it depending on your settlement; however, you will want to be prepared either way.

Well-Being of the Children

The well-being of the children is imperative in your *Conscious Divorce.* Their emotional and physical security will be of the utmost importance. It will also be the responsibility of you and your spouse to protect the children from the emotional challenges that the divorce process will bring. Lastly, make sure they know that the divorce is not their fault and that they are loved. These are the two most important issues for children in divorce.

Emotional distress and challenges are almost unavoidable in divorce – for all involved. However, mindfully preparing and setting intentions will help to reduce the overall emotional distress.

In divorce, being mindful about your needs and deliberate with your preparations is important. Many of these preparations may take place discreetly over time. Implement a strategy that works for you, however long it takes. Move forward and only execute the divorce when you are prepared.

Sometimes during *The Preparations* phase of divorce people get "cold feet." The fear of what lies ahead really settles in. There may be moments where you feel that the known, and your current unhappiness, are better than the unknown and your chance of happiness. Your feelings and emotions will fluctuate; but, do not use these as your guidance system in this phase of divorce. Stay mindful and conscious of why you are doing this and what your overall goal is. It is a challenging process; however, your happiness and freedom are what is at stake. This is about *You Choosing You*! Stay focused on your intentions: to prepare for your happiness and freedom.

> *To be prepared is half the victory.*
>
> **- Miguel De Cervantes**

Loose Lips Sink Ships

Gossip can undermine your efforts.

One thing that became apparent to me during my divorce preparations was how important it was to keep my intentions to divorce and my family affairs as private as possible. Not only did I want to be the one to inform my former husband of my decision, but also, I wanted to do it when I was prepared to do so and not a moment sooner. The same was the case with my daughter. It was imperative that she was informed of this decision by her parents and no one else. With this in mind, privacy was instrumental during the divorce.

Loose lips can indeed sink ships. Maintaining my privacy was extremely challenging, especially in a time where I really needed the support and ear of a good friend. At the time of my decision to divorce, I confided in a counsellor and a friend who lived out of town and was out of my immediate friend circle. These mindful decisions saved my family and me from potential emotional distress. In addition, the discreteness that I displayed was instrumental in my successful preparations for the divorce.

Having the self-discipline and self-respect to keep our affairs private is often neglected, especially with the prevalence of social media. Privacy allows you to choose your thoughts and feelings and with whom you want to share them. So, for all aspects of life, make sure that what you are saying and sharing serves you and hurts no one.

Never announce your moves before you make them.

- fabQuote.com

PRINCIPLE 17

Refuse to Play the Game

The Game of Life can be a drama unless
you refuse to play.

Divorce can give you a lot of emotional drama to deal with: from the shifting emotional stances of you and your spouse, to the opinions and fears of others, to the judgements of society. However, divorce is a personal decision of responsibility from deep within us. So, remain grounded in your decision and intentions throughout the phases of divorce regardless of any outside drama.

Many of my family members and friends shared their opinions about my divorce and sometimes offered me unsolicited advice. This is to be expected to some degree. However, I was surprised – and even shocked – by the snarls and comments of mere acquaintances who judged a situation they knew very little about. In addition, there are still societal biases about how women should commit to their marriage and *not* choose themselves.

During my divorce, I found that it was easier to dismiss the comments and opinions of others about my divorce, than it was to deal with my former husband and the emotional game of chess that took place between us. One resource that helped me deal with my marital relationship during the divorce process was David Emerald's *The Power of TED*, which explains the game of the *drama triangle* and how to no longer play it!

The *Power of TED* really broadened my understanding of relationships and the roles we play in them. In our relationships, most of us will play one of these roles: *rescuer, persecutor or victim,* while the other partner plays the counter role to the one we are playing. We will shift from role to role, depending upon the stance of the other. It's a game of drama and codependency. A typical progression of these roles would be the following: *You rescue someone from a situation. You become resentful for having rescued them so you persecute them. You feel like a victim because you were not appreciated.* The opposing roles to this progression would be: *You appear to be a victim who needs rescuing. You feel persecuted, like a victim, because you were helped, but with resentment. You become angry and you persecute the other for their insult to your capabilities.*

A relationship could go on and on in this triangular pattern, with the partners feeding off of each other and taking on counter roles. This triangle is also a game of dis-empowerment and unworthiness that continues until you decide to stop and leave the triangle and no longer play the game. After many years in the triangle with my former husband, as well as other relationships in my life, I eventually left all triangles and stopped playing the game. Learning how to no longer play this emotional game saved me from a lot of drama during the divorce process. No reacting. No drama. This contributed to a more stable environment for the entire family during our divorce.

Reacting to others contributes to emotional drama in our relationships. In addition, trying to meet the expectations of others can feel self-defeating, like a game you cannot win, or at least a game you are tired of playing. I know I was! So, instead of playing the games, remain aware and consciously choose to pause and respond to life instead of reacting to life! Your awareness and mindfulness will allow you to see the games and then make different choices. In the end, it preserves energy and attention for what really matters, what's actually your responsibility, and what you can control, *you and your choices!*

> *Don't be fooled. People who create drama and then portray themselves as the victim are playing games. They are manipulating you.*
>
> **- SwanWaters.com**

The Process

You will find that you don't need to trust others as much as you need to trust yourself to make the right choices.

—Don Miguel Ruiz

During *The Process* phase of divorce it's imperative to "keep your cool." The *Principles* included in this section help support a calmer and more focused you, so that you can effectively make empowering decisions during this phase.

PRINCIPLE 18

Offer the Gift of Grace

Grace is the kindness and love we offer when our
ego is out of the way.

One of the key intentions that I had for my divorce was to offer *grace*! The process of divorce is an emotional rollercoaster; we never really know how the other is going to behave, and the unknown is around every corner. The one thing I *did* know was that I had control over how I would behave. Grace is a choice and I chose to offer grace whenever I could. We have the ability to offer someone our kindness and love, even when we believe they are undeserving of it in the moment.

My ability to offer grace, to choose peace over being right, worked for the benefit of my entire family. I valued taking the least destructive divorce route possible. Because my former husband, my daughter, and I all resided together during the divorce process, *I chose* to remove my ego in many instances and to allow only the truth to remain. I made the decision to divorce for my own self-worth and completing the divorce in order to start my new life was the goal. That's it! No ego, no malice, just facts. This allowed me to choose grace.

If we are able to offer grace to others, it's a blessing for us as well. When we understand that we all have our moments of egoic struggle, and we offer grace, we are seeing the love in the other and also in ourselves. Our egos hide who we really are. In our EGO we *Edge God Out*. So, the next time you are challenged by someone's egoic confrontation, before you react ask yourself, *"What would love do?"* That is grace.

> *You can either be a host to God or a host to your ego. It's your call.*
>
> **- Wayne Dyer**

Treat Others as You Want to Be Treated

The Golden Rule – Do unto others as you would have others do unto you.

I have always believed in this *Principle*; and the importance of it was validated during my divorce. There were many times during my divorce process where I was emotionally triggered, and therefore tempted to react in a vindictive way towards my former husband. Instead, I embraced the *Golden Rule!*

My efforts to live the *Golden Rule* were not based on the intention of being kind to my former husband – that was just a positive side effect of this *Principle*. I used the *Golden Rule* to hold onto my own dignity and integrity. I refused to lose myself during this process or to become a woman who I did not respect or value.

The *Golden Rule* is truly the most poignant, effective and revealing *Principle*. If only we could all make an oath to treat other people exactly how we would like to be treated, in all circumstances, it would alleviate so much turmoil and hate in the world. In addition, the *Golden Rule* actually reveals to us how we view ourselves. *Do unto others as you would have others do unto you* has more of a literal translation than you may realize. How we treat others mirrors how we perceive ourselves. With this understanding, this *Principle* is a window into our perception of our own worth. It gauges how much we are loving ourselves. Each time I had a gracious or kind response, it revealed to me the worth and self-love I did have for myself.

This *Principle* also revealed to me areas about myself that needed my attention and awareness, such as my judgements and lack of patience. Not only was my character challenged in these areas when it came to others, but also, I realized I was harsh with myself in these areas as well. The *Golden Rule* gives us an awareness of our own selves. Because of this, I am now more mindful of having acceptance and patience with myself, and therefore with others.

Be mindful of how you treat others *and* how you treat yourself. You will surely find a direct correlation between the two. Treat others with love and respect and feel that energy for yourself as well. Be kind and gentle to yourself, and be a gift to others.

> *The way people treat you is a statement about who they are as a human being. It is not a statement about you.*
>
> **- Anonymous**

PRINCIPLE 20

Choose Compassion

Compassion for others is an act of self-love and understanding.

There will be nothing more challenging than granting yourself, as well as your spouse, compassion during the divorce process. All that has led up to this point needs to be accepted. All that you have experienced and are experiencing has made you who you are. Allow yourself to see it all from a place of understanding, gentleness and self-love. Treat yourself with kindness because you are your own best friend. Treat your spouse with understanding because he or she is also experiencing the same pain and changes that you are experiencing. There are always two sides to every coin and sometimes we can't see the other side – but it does exist.

Compassion will allow you to move through the divorce process with more peace in your soul. Just be careful to not translate compassion into feelings of pity and sadness for your spouse. If you allow him or her to become the victim and you the persecutor, guilt is often the result. This could jeopardize your efforts. There is a fine line between understanding and pity. Compassion empowers you both, pity disempowers you both.

During my divorce I considered how the decisions I made affected my former husband. I held an understanding for what he was going through. I was kind and considerate to him as much as I could be during such a trying time. However, I never allowed his pain to become mine. I would not accept his emotional responsibility, only an understanding of it. Choosing compassion allowed me to show grace and kindness while still *choosing myself*. It allowed me to feel love and respect for myself and stay true to my intentions of taking the higher road for the overall well-being of my family.

Compassion is such a necessary human trait in a world riddled with judgement and hate. How we treat others is a reflection of how we view ourselves; therefore, it is important to have compassion for each other. When we offer love and understanding to another, we are expressing our own self-love. We empower ourselves as well as the other. Compassion followed by acts of kindness is the most empowering act of all. Implement compassion into your life and witness more peace, love and joy along your journey.

Do things for people not because of who they are or what they do in return, but because of who you are.

- Harold Kushner

PRINCIPLE 21

Fear Is a Choice

Fear is caused by a belief, so change your belief.

Fear was the strongest emotion I experienced throughout the entire process of divorce. It was the one emotion that could have stopped me dead in my tracks, if it was not for my courage.

Fear has the ability to keep us trapped in a psychological and emotional prison, where we believe that we are unable to affect change or take effective action. You may have heard the acronym for FEAR as *False Evidence Appearing Real*. This acronym is so powerful because it reveals the truth about fear – it is caused by our beliefs. Although feeling fear is valid, your beliefs that cause you to feel fear may not be valid. We can release our fears about something when we change or question our belief about it. What do we believe that may not actually be true? Are these beliefs *our* beliefs or did they originate from someone else?

My greatest fear was that I would not be able to successfully complete the divorce process. I worried about all of the unknown factors that were ahead – from financial instability to loneliness, from future happiness to the hope of a loving, future relationship – and of course, the effect of the divorce on my daughter.

Fear can lead to self-destructive behaviors. The unconscious ways in which I dealt with fear and anxiety negatively affected me. It added great stress to both my mental and physical bodies. Fear caused me to believe that I was not safe and could no longer trust my place in my world. This led me to isolate myself and feel lonely. This belief also led me to overeat and gain 30 pounds. This weight provided me with a sense of shelter and protection from the world. Lastly, fear led me to overindulge in alcohol in an attempt to find relief from the pain and fear. These painful consequences came from my unconscious reaction to fear.

You will move through your divorce process more peacefully when you become aware of the fear, move through it, and choose effective methods to deal with it. Many of the *Principles* in this book will help you move through your fears. *Principle 10 – The ABCs of Decision Making* – suggests that you apply awareness to your thoughts and question the validity of your beliefs since they may be causing fear. *Principle 11 – Let Your Faith be Greater than Your Fear* – encourages you to move beyond your fearful, limiting beliefs into courageous, faithful action. *Principle 12 – Affirmations Allow Transformation* – offers you affirming thoughts to replace your fearful beliefs so that you can courageously take action towards what you desire.

Essentially, everything that we fear is really a thought about the absence of what we desire. Fear is the worry that what we truly desire will not happen. Just beyond every fear is that desire. They are two ends of the same stick. Focus on what you desire, and believe that you can accomplish your goals!

As President Franklin D Roosevelt said, *"The only thing to fear is fear itself."* Fear is a choice, and when we allow it in, it infiltrates our life. It creates our limitations and how we perceive our reality.

I hope that you will take time to become aware of and release your fears. The more courage you have, the less fear you will experience. When you perceive fear as a choice, you understand that you can control it and you can shift it. Without fear, you stop creating your own prison and limitations. You become free and limitless!

> *Whatever you fear most has no power. It is your fear that has the power.*
>
> **- Oprah Winfrey**

Practice Emotional Intelligence

_____

The ability to control your emotions allows you to have peace and stability.

If there was ever a time in my life when I needed to have control over my emotions, it was during my divorce. It is truly an emotional rollercoaster: from wanting to cry in devastation one moment, to feeling full-on rage the next. Remaining aware of my emotional state and trying my best to breathe through it was not only for my benefit, but also for the benefit of all involved. The fewer extreme emotional reactions I displayed, the more stable and effective I was in dealing with the divorce process, and the more peace there was in our household.

I used many tactics in order to effectively manage my emotions during the divorce process. This is *emotional intelligence.* The following tools will hopefully serve you in maintaining emotional intelligence as much as they served me:

1. *The Pause* – If you intentionally pause for a number of breaths before reacting to anything, it greatly decreases the chances of reacting in an emotional or unconscious manner. This will allow you to consciously respond.

2. *Thoughts Create Emotions* – Your emotions are usually the result of a story you are telling yourself. When you are emotional, *stop* the momentum by *stopping the story.* If you stop your attachment to the story and become present, you may return to a less emotional state.

3. *Know Yourself* – Many people are consciously aware of their own emotional triggers. So, before entering into any situation that may activate a trigger, prepare yourself with awareness and an

intention to stop it. Awareness transforms. Know your triggers and choose to respond – not react!

4. *It Takes Two to Tango* – If your spouse wishes to engage in an altercation with you, simply choose not to engage. Remove yourself from the space or have a response prepared that dismisses you from the interaction, such as "I will not discuss this with you." Then walk away. This is one you can use if your spouse wants to "discuss" divorce-related items that are better dealt with through your lawyers.

5. *Use Emotional Outlets* – It is important that you take the time and find a safe space to decompress and ground yourself throughout the divorce process. Take time for exercise, yoga, meditation, nature walks, reading a book, taking a bath, listening to music, having a spa treatment, shopping, doing something creative and reread your *Divorce Mission Statement*. Lastly, get rest! A rested you is a less emotional you! Be willing to supply yourself with compassion and TLC as a priority, in order to maintain the focus and stamina you need for this process.

6. *Find Support* – Have that comforting person and ear available to you for when you need it. Whether it is a counsellor, a family member or a close friend, having someone you trust as a confidant, preferably outside of your marital circle, will help you survive divorce.

Emotional intelligence helps life flow more smoothly. Don't mistake emotional intelligence for repressing emotions – they are not the same. Emotional intelligence is an understanding and conscious awareness of our emotions. It also includes the responsibility to heal our emotions, in order to effectively manage our energy. We all need to feel, as you will read under *Principle 25, You Must Feel to Heal.* However, in a time where stability, focus and effectiveness are needed, emotional intelligence provides us with a solution.

Don't let your emotions distract you from what needs to be done. Control your emotions or your emotions will control you.

- livehappy.com

Boundaries Are an Act of Self-Love

Boundaries allow us to commit to relationships,
starting with the relationship with ourselves.

Boundaries are something that I did not have in my life, until my divorce. I saw myself as someone people could rely on, depend on, lean on. Unfortunately, every so often someone took advantage of me because I did not know how to set boundaries, or even that it was necessary to do so. I was a people pleaser, which attracted Narcissistic personalities into my life. It became obvious that something needed to change because this was no longer supporting my well-being.

While boundaries initially appear to be something that would put a wedge in a relationship, in the end, it's just the opposite. True friendships and relationships thrive with boundaries in place. Boundaries are just a mindful declaration of what you will or will not do. Boundaries are limits that support your commitments to yourself, while still being able to make commitments to others. This clarity and understanding between individuals allows for the relationship to thrive. When a relationship cannot survive your boundaries, it likely means that these individuals are not willing to honor you and probably are not aware of their own boundaries.

Setting boundaries for the divorce will be necessary. Especially with the number of people and opinions that will be coming your way. Boundaries may mean saying no to invitations or keeping people out of your personal affairs. Some boundaries are for others, while some may be for your own self control. Most importantly, you may find yourself setting new boundaries in your relationship with your spouse during this process. It may be necessary to say no to something you have always said yes to in the past.

You may also need to redefine your role as a spouse during the divorce process, and this will include new boundaries. It will be important, now more than ever, that *You Choose You* over anyone else. This commitment to yourself is a form of self-love.

For me, boundaries became more about rebuilding the relationship that I had with myself than with anyone else. I was living authentically and honoring my desires. Learning to *Choose Myself* was a new type of commitment, and one that I now highly value. Boundaries help maintain a feeling of safety, ease and trust in relationships. However, I learned that the relationship that needs the most trust is the one with yourself!

> *Daring to set boundaries is about having the courage to love ourselves, even when we risk disappointing others.*
>
> **- Brene Brown**

PRINCIPLE 24

Intuition Is Your Superpower

Your intuition is where you find your answers.

Throughout the overwhelming experience of divorce I quickly realized that I needed to remain grounded and acutely aware of every decision I had to make and every action I was taking. There were times when important decisions had to be made while I was feeling intense emotions. There were also times when I sought, or was "volunteered," the opinions of others, which only added to the complexity of these decisions. At the end of the day, I knew I valued one thing above all else, my own opinion, my own knowing. To make my decisions with clarity, I needed to hear my own voice the loudest – my inner voice. A friend once described this as *intuition* and it is true.

In order to hear, feel and understand your own knowing, instincts or intuition, you may need to slow down and just *be still*. This may require secluding yourself and meditating. Even in the midst of the divorce I knew these decisions had to be made in conscious awareness, with intuition. That whisper of knowing inside of you is *your superpower*. I had to find those moments where I could slow down and quiet the barrage of thoughts going through my mind. I had to learn how to hear and trust my intuition again. Self-trust added to my empowerment, and I would not have made it through my divorce sanely without reconnecting to my intuition!

You may find that as you intentionally take moments to slow down and be still, you will be able to hear and use the innate intelligence of your intuition. I highly recommend meditation to help you accomplish this. If you do not already know how to, do some research on ways to meditate. Because when we use our superpower of intuition, we can more easily access the answers we need for *all* decisions we make in life.

> *Intuition is your soul whispering the truth to your heart and hoping that you hear.*
>
> **- Kate Spencer**

A New Story for a New Beginning

Are there things in your life that are as you want them to be? Keep telling that story.

Are there things in your life that are not as you want them to be? Don't tell that story.

Look and speak in the direction of where you want to be, not where you are or where you were.

- Abraham Hicks

A New Beginning

The secret to change is to focus all of your energy
not on fighting the old, but on building the new.

- Socrates

The *Principles* in this final phase are all focused on how to support your healing – your self-love – and how to live your best life. It's a period of reflection and release. It's a time for acceptance and self-love. It's a journey of authenticity.

PRINCIPLE 25

You Must Feel to Heal

Healing includes feeling and
releasing your emotions.

After the upheaval of the divorce process has come to an end, and you have begun to create your new beginning, there is relief and finally some peace. Now it is time to allow for reflection and healing. Healing will allow you to create and rebuild your life on more solid ground. It's important that you create your new beginning from a stable, mindful and grounded state. Give yourself this gift! Sometimes, after divorce, we are so excited about our new found freedom that we jump into new activities only to find that we need to retreat and allow for time and space to fully heal.

After my divorce, I found myself in a full-on adventure, doing all the things and living all the life that I had *not* during the last few years of my marriage. After a year, I came circling back to finish the internal reflection and emotional release that would allow me to mindfully create the next part of my journey. I took time to ask: *How am I evolving from here and what do I want to create for my future?* I needed to accept and make peace with my decision to divorce. I knew I needed to feel compassion for myself and be proud of myself. But most of all, I needed to *feel to heal!*

What does healing look like? In order to become aware of the wounds that need healing, you must take time to *be still.* Just as you are taking responsibility for other areas in your life, you must take responsibility for your healing. Become aware of and own your wounds that need healing. Then you have the ability to release and heal those wounds, in order to start anew.

How do you feel? I took the time to feel angry and then sad, to grieve and then comfort myself. I also took the time to look deeply at all that I had learned, especially about myself, through the experience of divorce. Allow yourself time to reflect and become aware so that you grow through this process.

Feeling our emotions can be an overwhelming experience; and many of us deny and repress emotions for much of our lives to avoid feeling their intensity. However, once we have the courage to feel and release, in a place where we feel safe, we give ourselves the greatest gift – freedom. We make more space within ourselves for the positive and loving emotions that we truly desire. For me, the joy of being free from my repressed emotions far outweighed the fear of feeling them. It may be the same for you as well, and one of the greatest gifts you can give yourself – internal acceptance, peace and freedom!

During my healing process, I found that I was healing wounds from my entire life, not just the divorce. The divorce became the event that allowed me, finally, to go in and see what was truly going on in my inner world. I saw some of my own life patterns and choices more clearly – who I allowed in, how I interacted with people, where my boundaries were or were not and what my limiting beliefs were. I asked myself questions:

Which of my choices have been disempowering?

What did I believe about my worth and value?

When did these beliefs and patterns begin?

Where did they come from?

Are they true?

Taking the time to answer these questions for myself was the key to healing my wounds and creating a better future. I allowed the answers to provide me with clarity, understanding, and a new perspective of my past experiences, and therefore a new platform in which to build my future. We can go through this process of healing on our own or with the support of a coach or therapist.

We usually have more healing to do than we realize; and it usually takes longer than we think it will. This was certainly my experience. However, this inner work allows us to rebuild from a place of greater strength and stability, knowing ourselves more authentically. After all, *Everywhere You Go there You Are!* So, feel, release the past, and heal so that you can evolve and start again from a new and healthier place. And as you do, be mindful of having that solid foundation upon which to build your new life. That foundation is *you*!

Our deepest powers lay in our ability to feel. The deeper one is willing to feel – the deeper one can transform, heal, mature and manifest in this life. It's through feeling that we commune and dance with the intelligence of existence. It's through feeling that we come to know our Godliness.

- Chris Bale

Forgiveness Is for You

When you forgive someone you free yourself.

There are two sides to every story. When a marriage ends in divorce, both sides may carry some resentment, anger or blame towards the other, but you can only control your side. So, when the dust has settled, and you are moving forward with your life, the last thing you want to do is carry painful and self-destructive feelings with you. Resentment and anger are a prison and a burden that attach you negatively to another person. You chose divorce to be free, so offer forgiveness and *be free* – for you.

After the divorce was final, I was free from a marriage that was not working; but, it took much longer to free myself from my own mental prison. It was hard to let go of the limiting beliefs, the feelings of emptiness, the pain, and the rage. Physically I had moved on, but emotionally I was still processing the entire thing. I wanted to forgive, but there was a part of me that did not know how to let it go. It can be confusing to understand the difference between the *idea* of forgiving someone and *actually* forgiving someone – releasing emotions and feeling free from the associated pain. There are a handful of insights that helped me to free myself and let forgiveness in. These insights may also help you release the burden of these emotions:

It Isn't About You

All that appears to have been done to or against you actually has nothing to do with you and everything to do with them. Their actions are about them and their journey – not yours. Understanding this allows you to no longer attach their actions to you personally.

Suffering is Optional

The heavy energy that you may feel inside is optional. It is not hurting anyone but you. We all feel pain, hurt, etc. We all need to process these feelings. However, the past is the past. Are you holding onto its pain even though it no longer exists? Stop believing that this pain is yours to carry. Focus on the present moment and choose to let the past go.

Choose You!

Instead of wasting your energy being *against* someone, rechannel it and use it *for* yourself! *Choose you* and your freedom. Put your energy into doing things you love and that feed your soul.

See the Gifts

In most challenging situations there is a *life lesson*. Taking responsibility for all of your life experiences will offer you the opportunity to transform difficult experiences into lessons, wisdom and gifts. When you consciously accept these gifts you allow forgiveness.

Applying these insights really helped me shift my perspective and energy, and let the past dissolve away.

Once I accepted that the events of the past were long gone, and my part in them, I began to heal and forgive. I had to allow myself the freedom of the present moment where, with humility and understanding, I could choose to learn from the past and find peace. In the end, the past only exists in our minds. So start a new story in present time, where all of the power of choice, freedom and creation takes place.

Even after all of that, there was one element still missing. I still had to forgive the most important person in the story – *me*! I had to forgive myself for giving away my power, which was the root of my resentment, and not taking responsibility for my happiness. I had to show myself compassion. Realizing this was the most freeing moment of all; I now had to allow myself the freedom to create my life anew.

As you use these tools in your own life to forgive, you will experience more freedom. When we accept responsibility for our experiences and the gifts they bring, we understand that life is a continuous lesson, with nothing but forgiveness and understanding to be gained! When we take complete responsibility for our own journey and release others from being responsible for our experiences, we may realize that forgiveness is not even needed. Overall, we are here to *enjoy the journey* and embrace our evolution.

In the end, freedom has allowed my former husband and me to evolve our relationship, to become considerate to each other and form a new friendship as we co-parent our daughter.

> *To forgive is to set a prisoner free and to discover that the prisoner was you.*
>
> **- Lewis Smedes**

You're the One You've Been Waiting For

———————

You have the ability to give yourself
everything that you need.

If there is one thing that my divorce forced me to look at, it was my ability to care for and about myself in all ways. As a stay at home mom for many years, financial security was a predominant need and a major concern. However, I also lacked other areas of self-care in my life. I would not consider myself a needy person. I view myself as a strong, independent woman. But, upon reflection, I see that

I chose to be a victim when I was disappointed about not receiving the attention, love, or recognition that I desired from my husband. No one else knew; but I felt sadness and a deep void inside of me as these needs went unmet.

I also wanted to *be* needed. I was often the person who excessively met the needs of others. I realized that I would try to *prove my worth* to them and to myself. Filling other's needs more than my own exhausted me and created resentment.

I also realized that only I held the responsibility to make the changes for myself that I desired. With this awareness, I began to transform these needs into gifts that I now give to myself- "me time," self-care, self-love and self-gratitude.

Slowly, I supplied myself with what I needed in order to fill that void. I even began to buy myself roses every week as a reminder of my appreciation for beauty. They made *me* feel beautiful. This and other rituals became part of a growing self-care routine of love and wholeness that I embraced. However, I had to learn how to implement these new acts of self-care with love instead of judgement towards myself. As a result, I no longer waited for someone else to fill my bucket. I now fill it on my own – I actively provide myself with love. After all, I finally understand that I am the love of my life, and *you* are the love of yours! As Byron Katie so eloquently stated in her book, *I Need Your Love - Is that True?* - you're the one you've been waiting for!

We all desire connection with and love from others. This is what makes us feel alive – it's part of being human. However, we can accept love and attention from others as the "frosting on the cake," while we supply ourselves with what we need – our commitment to our own love and well-being. When we empower and appreciate ourselves – that we truly are our own answers – that *we are enough* – then we can graciously accept whatever others share with us. It allows for more gratitude, freedom and acceptance in relationships.

I used to hope that you'd bring me flowers.
Now I plant my own.

- Rachel Wolchin

PRINCIPLE 28

Unconditional Love Is True Freedom

When you love yourself and others without
conditions it frees you to live authentically.

One of the most enlightened realizations I had about my marriage was that I was in a marriage of conditional love. Many of us unknowingly live in conditional relationships and marriages. We have expectations of one another, and sometimes these may not be in alignment with what the other desires for themselves. When this is the case, the more we deny our desires, and ignore our wants and needs, the more we lose our authenticity. Many times we voluntarily betray ourselves to meet the needs of others, and then resent them as a result. We may even unconsciously withhold our love from the other, in resentment. Our love for others then becomes conditional and is based on meeting expectations in return for love. We may offer ourselves conditional love as well, possibly feeling regret for not meeting our own expectations.

Expectations seem to be a part of most relationships. When they become a prerequisite for love, it is a problem. Knowing and understanding each other's expectations and intentions may allow for a more harmonious relationship. However, if expectations are not met, respect and acceptance is still needed. It is important to understand that each person is ultimately responsible for his or her own happiness. It is not the responsibility of one person to please another, nor does anyone have the right to control the conditions or actions of another in order to fulfill their own desires. Ultimately, it is knowing what you are responsible for controlling – yourself!

When we learn to love unconditionally – and not hold another accountable for our own happiness – we will have the wonderful freedom to live authentically with one another. We can then appreciate and celebrate each other's individuality within the relationship. True love is being in a relationship where we are both responsible for our own well-being and are in alignment with who we really are – where we love each other without forfeiting love for ourselves. This means that we each need to love ourselves unconditionally *first*. This is both of us saying, *I Choose Me!* Only then can we choose the relationship unconditionally. *That* is a *Conscious Relationship! That* is *Unconditional Love* – for each other – as well as for ourselves!

> *I find the best way to love someone is not to change them, but instead help them reveal the greatest version of themselves.*
>
> **- Dr. Steve Maraboli**

PRINCIPLE 29

Allow Good Vibes Only

Energy can either support or hinder our well-being.

The energy that surrounds us has a direct effect on our well-being. If we are not aware of the energy that surrounds us, and the energy that we take into our physical bodies, we can feel heavy, sick and upset without understanding why.

Particularly during the end of my marriage and divorce, I felt the negative energy that existed all around me; although for years I had felt the effects of negative energy on my body both mentally and physically. As a result, I knew for sure that from then on, I would live this *Principle* and only allow good vibrations and good energy into my life.

During the difficult years in my marriage, I suppressed and trapped so many negative thoughts and so much negative energy in my body that I became physically ill. When the negative energy from painful experiences becomes repressed or trapped within us, it not only affects our thoughts and abilities to respond to life, but also, it can hurt our physical body and cause disease –"dis-ease." Therefore, you must become your own security system – regulating, choosing and *allowing only good vibes* into your life! In addition, remember to let yourself *feel to heal* and release your negative emotions so that you can support your well-being!

The feelings of joy, peace, gratitude and love help heal us and support mental and physical well-being. Thoughts that are uplifting support our emotions and our body's innate ability to heal itself. Therefore, choose thoughts, emotions, places and activities that bring you these positive feelings and vibrations.

The environment that I created in my new home, post-divorce, was one of peace, love and harmony. It was an environment full of positive vibrations where I could feel safe and heal. I reminded myself daily that there was *always* something for which to be grateful, and consciously worked towards becoming a contributor of positive and loving energy in the world, as much as welcoming it.

Sending good vibrations and energy *into* the world is the other half of the responsibility of energy. Managing the vibrations in your life can serve all. Whenever possible, release negative thoughts and emotions, and embody positive thoughts and emotions. The energy will follow. Allow only good vibrations into your life and become a source of positive light for the world. In the end, this will attract good vibrations back to you. After all, *like attracts like*.

> *Gratitude can transform any situation. It alters your vibration, moving you from negative energy to positive.*
>
> **- Oprah Winfrey**

PRINCIPLE 30

When You Change, Your Reality Changes

Your reality is a reflection of your beliefs and your energetic vibration.

So many things about my reality changed after my divorce. Places held new meanings. People I knew felt different and had different energy. My priorities shifted. My desires were new. Let's face it – I was different! I had different energy! I was the common denominator in all of this.

After *growing* through all that I had experienced in my marriage and divorce, after healing so many past wounds, I *was* a different person. I had allowed myself to evolve. My beliefs about who I was in the world and what was important to me had transformed. I became a more authentic, and therefore, more confident version of myself. This has been my evolution of courage and consciousness. This is the version of myself that I love. As I evolve and change, so does my reality. If we allow it, we are always in a state of becoming and evolving. It is a conscious choice we make each day.

Whenever we work to transform our beliefs into ones that better serve us, we will automatically see this reflected in our reality. When our beliefs and choices align us with our highest potential, it allows us to live consciously and become the person we desire. Or, we can live passively and unconsciously, forfeiting the ability to create our best selves. Through personal responsibility for my thoughts, beliefs, choices and actions, I now consciously create myself and my journey. I am no longer a passive, unconscious participant in my life.

Through divorce I have come to realize that endings are just new beginnings – and life is essentially a series of endings and beginnings. And while it is what it is, it always becomes what you make it! So, live consciously and deliberately, and create *a new story for a new beginning!* Be courageous and kind to yourself and others! Show up for your life! Take responsibility for your journey and empower yourself to create a life you will love! You are the one you've been waiting for, so celebrate yourself and keep saying, *I Choose Me!* Then you can be a light that empowers others.

Be the change you wish to see in the world.

- Gandhi

Conclusion

Divorce, like all adversities in life, can bring you to your knees. The process of divorce was one of the most painful and difficult experiences I have ever had. Divorce challenges what you are made of in all ways. It can break you or it can transform you – but the choice is yours. I chose to transform.

Responsibility and choice became my main tools of empowerment throughout my divorce, and I continue to use them in my life today. The divorce challenged me to take a new level of responsibility for my life and my happiness, and for this I am grateful. Taking responsibility meant making mindful choices for myself. I chose to have the courage to divorce with compassion for all. I chose to make conscious decisions throughout the divorce and to grow through my experience.

Beginning again, I have created a life of love, acceptance and empowerment, attracting wonderful people and experiences into my life. Everyday I consciously remind myself to *Choose Me!*

The woman who made the choice to divorce four years ago would be proud of who I have become today. The wisdom that I gained from the experience of my divorce has allowed me to better understand myself and to take full responsibility for the remainder of my journey. It has transformed who I am and empowered me to become fearless. It has provided me with a new understanding of freedom. Today I am free from self-imprisonment and from the internal suffering of living inauthentically. When we align with our *Truth*, we find clarity and freedom, we feel empowered and happy, and life becomes limitless.

My experience has given me a new appreciation for everything in life. We never stop learning, growing or becoming. In the end, divorce became another opportunity to choose self-love and evolve – one of the many I will experience in life. Time can heal, so there is hope! But you must choose to grow and transform through your divorce so that you can live a conscious life that you love. The choice is yours – *Choose You* and evolve!

I will conclude by sharing these wise words from Mother Teresa. They direct us to go within – to realize that our greatest responsibility is to live a life of authenticity. Our *ultimate* responsibility is to God. Mother Teresa's words remind us to live our Truth, regardless of what others do. May these words ground and uplift you.

DO IT ANYWAY!

People are often unreasonable, irrational and self-centered.

FORGIVE THEM ANYWAY.

If you are kind, people may accuse
you of selfish, ulterior motives.

BE KIND ANYWAY.

If you are successful, you will win some unfaithful friends and some genuine enemies.

SUCCEED ANYWAY.

If you are honest and sincere,
people may deceive you.

BE HONEST AND SINCERE ANYWAY.

What you spend years creating,

others could destroy overnight.

CREATE ANYWAY.

If you find serenity and happiness,

some may be jealous.

BE HAPPY ANYWAY.

The good you do today, will often be forgotten.

DO GOOD ANYWAY.

Give the best you have, and it will never be enough.

GIVE YOUR BEST ANYWAY.

In the final analysis, *it is between you and God.*

IT WAS NEVER BETWEEN YOU AND

THEM ANYWAY!

- Mother Teresa

Acknowledgments

My lovely daughter for your courage to remain the kind and wonderful person that you are and for being the inspiration that drove me to seek a better way.

My former husband for the wonderful years of marriage and our beautiful daughter.

My grandmother, who passed after my divorce, for your unwavering love and kindness.

My parents and sisters for loving all versions of me, just as I am.

My friends who comforted and supported my daughter and me in our times of need.

My dog for adding fun and love to our lives.

My counselor and intuitive friend for your support and guidance.

My editor and soul-sister who helped me transform this book into it's best version.

My publisher and long-time friend who helped me bring this thought into reality.

The Universe/God for your love and guidance through the toughest journey of my life and allowing me the honor of sharing this wisdom with love.

APPENDIX A

The Principles

Principle 1

Choose Yourself

Have the courage to take responsibility for your own life journey.

Principle 2

Contrast Helps Clarity

Experiencing what you do not want brings more clarity about what you do want.

Principle 3

What You Resist Persists

When you resist the reality of something in your life, you only strengthen it.

Principle 4

Acceptance Is the Gateway to True Change

Acceptance of your reality empowers you to transform it.

Principle 5

Blaming Disempowers You

When you blame someone else you give them your power.

Principle 6

Live Authentically

Authenticity is being the person that your soul desires, and living the life you want to live.

Principle 7

Life Is Happening in the Present Moment

The only moment that truly exists is the present moment.

Principle 8

You Can't Lose What Truly Matters

You will always have everything that you will ever need inside of you.

Principle 9

Be the Example

We teach others who we are with our actions.

Principle 10

Use the ABCs of Decision Making

Awareness, Beliefs and Choices support decisions.

Principle 11

Let Your Faith Be Greater than Your Fear

Faith allows you to respond to life, fear does not.

Principle 12

Affirmations Allow Transformation

Affirmations allow us to become what we believe.

Principle 13

Intentions Matter

Your intentions are your personal mission statement.

Principle 14

Seek a Higher Perspective

When we see through the eyes of understanding, our perspective is always changed.

Principle 15

Be Prepared

For all things in life, prepare yourself for success.

Principle 16

Loose Lips Sink Ships

Gossip can undermine your efforts.

Principle 17
Refuse to Play the Game
The Game of Life can be a drama unless you refuse to play.

Principle 18
Offer the Gift of Grace
Grace is the kindness and love we offer when our ego is out of the way.

Principle 19
Treat Others as You Want to be Treated
The Golden Rule – Do unto others as you would have others do unto you.

Principle 20
Choose Compassion
Compassion for others is an act of self-love and understanding.

Principle 21
Fear is a Choice
Fear is caused by a belief, so change your belief.

Principle 22
Practice Emotional Intelligence
The ability to control your emotions allows you to have peace and stability.

Principle 23
Boundaries Are an Act of Self-Love
Boundaries allow us to commit to relationships, starting with the relationship with ourselves.

Principle 24
Intuition Is Your Superpower
Your intuition is where you find your answers.

Principle 25
You Must Feel to Heal
Healing includes feeling and releasing your emotions.

Principle 26
Forgiveness Is for You
When you forgive someone you free yourself.

Principle 27
You're the One You've Been Waiting For
You have the ability to give yourself everything that you need.

Principle 28
Unconditional Love Is True Freedom
When you love yourself and others without conditions it frees you to live authentically.

Principle 29

Allow Good Vibes Only

Energy can either support or hinder our well-being.

Principle 30

When You Change, Your Reality Changes

Your reality is a reflection of your beliefs
and your energetic vibration.

APPENDIX B

Empowering Quotes

---

*Courage is not the absence of fear, but rather the assessment
that something else is more important than fear.*

- Franklin D. Roosevelt

*You may not control all the events that happen to you,
but you can decide not to be reduced by them.*

- Maya Angelou

*One half of knowing what you want is knowing what you
must give up before you get it.*

- Sidney Howard

*Adversity in our life may seem like a problem, however,
adversity can make us grow and learn, an opportunity
that we may never have experienced. It all depends on
how you look at it.*

- Catherine Pulsifer

Accept what is, let go of what was, and have faith in what will be.

- Sonia Ricotti

One reason people resist change is because they focus on what they have to give up, instead of what they have to gain.

- Quotling.com

There are two ways to be. One is at war with reality. The other is at peace.

- Byron Katie

When you blame others you give up your power to change.

- Robert Anthony

Above all, be the heroine of your life, not the victim.

- Nora Ephron

There comes a point in life when you have to let go of all the pointless drama and all the people who create it.

- picturequotes.com

Beauty begins the moment you decide to be yourself.

- Coco Chanel

There are only two days in the year that nothing can be done. One is called yesterday and the other is called tomorrow. So today is the right day to love, believe, do and mostly live.

- Dalai Lama

Most humans are never fully present in the now because unconsciously they believe that the next moment must be more important than this one.

- Eckhart Tolle

Your vision will become clear only when you can look into your own heart. Who looks outside, dreams. Who looks inside, awakes.

- Carl Jung

Divorce isn't such a tragedy. A tragedy is staying in an unhappy marriage, teaching your children the wrong things about love. Nobody ever died of divorce.

- Jennifer Weiner

At any given moment you have two options: to step forward into growth, or back into safety.

- Abraham Maslow

To understand everything is to forgive everything.

- Buddha

Life is a matter of choices, and every choice you make makes you.

- John Maxwell

You don't become what you want, you become what you believe.

- Oprah Winfrey

Faith is unseen but felt, faith is strength when we feel we have none, faith is hope when all seems lost.

- Catherine Pulsifer

A constant realization of the presence of Spirit will provide a sense of divine companionship that no other attitude could produce.

- Ernest Holmes

This is the part where you find out who you are!

- Unknown

Before anything else, preparation is the key to success.

- Alexander Graham Bell

It is our attitude at the beginning of a difficult task which, more than anything else, will affect its successful outcome.

- William James

Privacy is power. What people don't know they can't ruin.

- The Mindsjournal

Sometimes it's better to react with no reaction.

- PictureQuotes

Grace is the atmosphere created by love that makes faith the only reasonable response.

- Bill Johnson

In the war of the ego, the loser always wins.

- Buddha

Love others to make them feel better and so that you see yourself in the mirrors of their eyes.

- Debasish Mridha

What you do not want done to yourself, do not do to others.

- Confucius

If you want others to be happy, practice compassion. If you want to be happy, practice compassion.

- Dalai Lama

Compassion becomes real when we recognize our shared humanity.

- Pema Chodron

Fear is not real. The only place that fear can exist is in our thoughts of the future.

- Will Smith

It is a product of our imagination causing us to fear things that do not at present and may not ever exist. That is near insanity. Danger is very real, but fear is a choice.

- Unknown

But instead of feeling safe and secure behind their armed walls they found themselves trapped in the prison they had built with their own fears.

- Katie J. Davis

Rather than being your thoughts and emotions, be the awareness behind them.

- Eckhart Tolle

Nothing ever goes away until it has taught us what we need to know.

- Pema Chodron

The only people who get upset about you setting boundaries are the ones who were benefiting from you having none.

- Anonymous

I believe in intuitions and inspirations. I sometimes feel that I am right. I do not know that I am.

- Albert Einstein

In order to love who you are, you cannot hate the experiences that shaped you.

- Andrea Dykitra

The past has no power over the present moment.

- Eckhart Tolle

May your inner voice be the kindest voice you know.

- Unknown

Self-respect, self-worth and self-love, all start with self. Stop looking outside of yourself for your value.

- Rob Liano

You don't need another person to make you whole. God already did that. Your job is to know it.

- Maya Angelou

Treat yourself the way you want others to treat you.
— Jennifer Pearce

Unconditional love is the outer expression of inner peace.
— Ponwell

Love is not rare. Unconditional love is.
— The Latest Quote

Be around people that are good for your soul.
— fabQuote.co

There is always something to be grateful for.
— Unknown

The more positive energy you throw into the universe, the more positive energy it gives you back.
— Nitin Namdeo

Freeing yourself was one thing. Taking responsibility for that freedom is another.
— Toni Morrison

Who you are tomorrow begins with what you do today.
— Tim Fargo

Resources

Beattie, Melody. *Codependent No More.*

Circle of Atonement. *A Course in Miracles: Based on the original handwritten notes of Helen Schucman and introductory material by Robert Perry.*

Eger, Edith. *The Gift.*

Emerald, David. *The Power of TED: The Empowerment Dynamic.*

Hawkins, David, M.D., Ph.D. *The Eye of the I, From Which Nothing is Hidden.*

Hawkins, David, M.D., Ph.D. *Truth vs Falsehood: How to Tell the Difference.*

Hicks, Abraham. *Abraham Hicks Daily,* Podcasts.

Hicks, Abraham. *Infinite Intelligence,* Podcasts.

Holmes, Ernest. *The Science of the Mind.*

Katie, Byron. *I Need Your Love - Is That True?*

Marciniak, Barbara. *Path of Empowerment.*

Tolle, Eckhart. *The Power of Now.*

Wightman, Nova. *Awake and Aligned.*

Made in the USA
Monee, IL
03 May 2023